TAKING CARE OF YOUR

CAT

Joyce Pope

Series consultant: Michael Findlay

**Photographs by: Sally Anne Thompson
and R T Willbie/Animal Photography**

Franklin Watts

London New York Toronto Sydney

The author

Joyce Pope is Enquiries Officer of the Zoology Department of the British Museum of Natural History and also gives regular public lectures to children and adults on a wide range of subjects.

She is involved with conservation groups and has written many books on a variety of topics including European animals, pets and town animals. She is an enthusiastic pet owner herself and currently keeps small mammals, two dogs, a cat and a horse.

The consultant

Michael Findlay is a qualified veterinary surgeon whose involvement has been mainly with pet animals. He is now an advisor to a pharmaceutical company. He is involved with Crufts Dog Show each year and is a member of the Kennel Club. He is president of several Cat Clubs and is Chairman of the Feline Advisory Bureau. He currently has three Siamese cats and two labrador dogs.

© 1986 Franklin Watts

First published in Great Britain in 1986 by
Franklin Watts
12a Golden Square
London W1

First published in the United States of America by
Franklin Watts Inc.
387 Park Avenue South
New York
N.Y. 10016

Printed in Belgium

UK edition:
ISBN 0 86313 364 9
US edition:
ISBN 0-531-10159-2
Library of Congress Catalog Card Number:
85-51605

Designed by
Ben White

Illustrated by
Hayward Art Group

Acknowledgments
The photographers and publishers would like to thank Mr. Neil Forbes of the Lansdown Veterinary Surgeons, Stroud, and the families and their cats who participated in the photographs for this book.

TAKING CARE OF YOUR

CAT

Contents

Introduction

People like to keep pets. They can be an interesting part of our lives. They can often be good company especially for someone who is alone or unwell. By watching and caring for pets, we can find out how other creatures use the world.

▽ The best sort of animal to keep as a pet is one that is not too large, but not so small that you cannot handle and stroke it safely. A pet should trust you and be able to return your affection.

Points to remember

You must remember that a pet is not a toy, which you can put away and forget, but a living creature like yourself. Like you it can be contented or afraid. It must have food, drink and a safe, warm place to sleep. It also needs exercise and play.

▽ In many ways cats are independent animals, yet they like the comforts that human beings can give them and they fit in very well with children and family life.

Cats make good pets

Cats are domestic animals, which means that, unlike wild animals, they are tame and not afraid of humans. It is a mistake to try and keep a wild animal, which probably would not be able to settle down with you and your family.

If you think that you would like to have a cat as a pet you must make sure that there is space for it in your house or apartment. A cat does not take up a lot of room, but it does need somewhere for its bed which will be a place that it can think of as its own.

▽ Cats love the warmth and comfort of a house, but many cats enjoy being out of doors. It is probable that your cat will hunt and catch birds and this can be almost impossible to stop. If you want to protect the wild birds you should put a bell on the cat's collar.

You must be sure that you can afford to keep a cat. The cost of feeding one would be a continous drain on your spending money. Also you must have your pet immunized every year against some serious cat diseases. You must be sure that you have the time to look after your cat, for it will need to be fed and taken care of every day.

You must have your parents' permission to keep a cat for you will almost certainly have to ask for their help sometimes – it is only fair that they should be consulted. Cats can live for a long time – they may survive for over 20 years – so keeping and caring for a cat will become a part of your way of life.

△ Although the cat may officially be your pet, it will probably play with the entire family. But you should be the one responsible for feeding and caring for it. Like all animals, cats are creatures of habit and you should try to feed it in the same place and at the same time each day. When it has eaten its food you should wash up the cat's dishes. These must be cleaned separately from the family's plates, cups and saucers.

Preparing to keep a cat

When you and your family have decided to keep a cat, there are some things that you must do before you can bring it home.

The cat's bed is the first thing to get ready. It may be a wicker basket, or made of plastic, a "bean bag" type of bed or even a cardboard box thickly lined with newspaper.

The bed should be big enough for the cat to stretch out in. Make sure it has a lining of blanket or warm material, which you can wash every week.

▷ Wherever you put the cat's bed, you should make sure that it is not in a draft. Cats seem to spend much of their lives asleep and if it does not like its bed or the place where you have put it, it may try to sleep on your furniture instead.

A cardboard box with a gap cut in one side so that the cat can get in easily is just as good as a more expensive sort of bed, but you must replace it if it gets worn or dirty.

Cats often want to come in and go out when there is nobody about to open the door for them. One way to let this happen is to fit a simple cat flap in the back door. A flap can be bought quite cheaply, but an adult should fit it.

Even if your cat can go outside, you should provide a litter box. There are many types but you should get one big enough for the cat to turn around in fairly easily.

As well as these things, you should buy a supply of food, a grooming kit and some toys before you bring your cat home.

△ Cats will not willingly soil the places in which they live. A litter box helps them to be clean, but you must play your part and check it every day, as a cat will not use a dirty litter box.

△ Cats quickly learn to use a cat flap fitted in a back or side door. For security, it can be locked at night.

△ Cats often roam but are more likely to be returned to you if they are wearing name tags on an elastic collar.

Choosing a cat

When you have decided that you really want a cat and have room and time for it, you then have to think about what sort you would like as a pet.

There are, like dogs, a great many cat breeds. Some have short coats, while others have very long hair.

▽ If you decide to have a pedigreed cat you will have to find somebody who breeds the variety that you want. Your parents or other adults should go with you, for most breeders will only sell to adults.

The long-haired cats may look very beautiful but you will need to spend a lot of time grooming them to keep their coats in good condition.

You may prefer your cat to be a particular color. You must also decide whether you want a male or a female. Unless you wish to breed from your cat, it should be neutered between the ages of six and nine months.

△ The wild ancestors of cats were tabbies, but there are now many colors to choose from. Cats which are the same color all over are called "solid colored". They may be black, white or various shades of grays and browns. Many red colored cats are males.

▷ Almost all tortoiseshell cats are female and have black and brown stripes or patches in their coats. Like this one, they may also have some white on their bodies. But though some breeds may be particular colors, the color alone does not affect the animal as a pet.

Cat breeds vary not only in general appearance but also in temperament and in hardiness. The long-haired breeds are often placid, but you may feel that the amount of time that you would need to spend on grooming each day would not make it a good pet for you.

The oriental breeds, generally long legged and short-coated, are often very beautiful but they may be high strung and demanding. Probably the best family pet is a short-haired variety, for these are usually playful and affectionate, as well as being quite healthy.

▽ Many domestic cats like this one, have medium long coats, which will not take as much grooming as a long-haired cat. The appearance of the parents will often give you an idea of what your kitten will look like when it is bigger.

△ Seal point Siamese cats are one of the favorite oriental breeds. They are affectionate but can often be rather noisy.

Whatever sort of breed you decide on, you should get an adult cat or a kitten aged between six and eight weeks old. Try to make your choice from a whole litter. The kittens should be lively and playful. If they are listless and not interested when you make a small noise they are probably unwell. You should not have one, for a sick kitten may not recover.

Check that the fur is in good condition, that noses are not runny and that eyes are bright and have no discharge. Choose a friendly kitten as this will make the best pet.

△ Persian cats are the best known long-haired breed. They are usually stockily built with very flat faces. The color of cats' eyes varies very greatly. Very young kittens often have blue eyes, but they may turn green or orange as they grow up.

◁ Burmese cats are most often the brown color shown here, but other colors, from lilac to tortoiseshell have been bred. They are agile and playful – many will retrieve balls or toys more like a dog than a cat and most are good hunters.

13

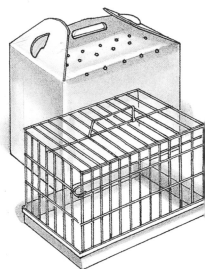

◁ A carrying case is important if you have a cat. You can use it for any journey, or when you have to take your pet to the vet. You will know that the cat is comfortable and safe in the case.

△ Here are two other types of carrying cases, made from cardboard and metal.

Wherever you get your cat, you will have to take it to your home. Try to do this on a day when you will have plenty of time to spend with it so that it can get to know you right away.

Even if you are going in a car, you must have a carrying case for the kitten as it could easily be frightened and escape from a car window. The case can be made of strong cardboard, metal or wood and wire mesh.

When you get home, take the case into the room where the cat's bed is. Make sure that the windows and doors are shut before you coax the kitten out. Offer it a drink of water or milk and let it explore one room. Don't forget to put a litter box in the room.

Your new pet can explore the rest of the house in the next few days, but it may become bewildered if there are too many new things for it to learn about all at once.

You can pick it up and play with it gently for a while, but a kitten will need to spend a lot of time asleep, so you should show it its bed as well.

△ When your kitten is exploring its new home, you should keep any other pets out of the room, so that it can gain confidence on its own.

Introduce other cats or dogs to it very carefully, a few days later.

Feeding your cat

Like all living creatures, cats need food, but they are meat eaters and cannot survive unless they eat meat. This can be given to them in all sorts of forms.

When you get your kitten you should find out what it is used to eating and how many meals a day it has been having. When it is full grown it will need only two meals per day.

▽ Here are some dishes you could use for feeding your cat. Never use the same dishes as your pets eat from. Fresh water must be put in a clean dish every day.

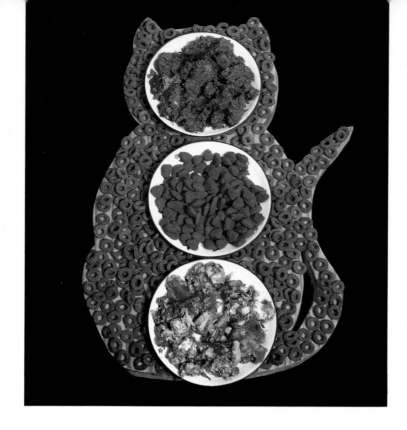

◁ *Top dish* contains canned food. This is the easiest type of diet to give your cat and you can get many flavors which will provide variety.
Middle dish contains semi dry food. This includes some vegetable protein and minerals and is cheaper than canned food.
Bottom dish contains cooked meat.
Cat shape shows dry food. This does not give an adequate diet and the cat must always have plenty of water to drink with it.

You should feed your cat at the same time and in the same place each day. You should use dishes that cannot easily be tipped over or broken. Make sure that they are not used for any other purpose.

You may want to feed your cat with fresh food, but it is better to cook it rather than serve it raw.

An easier way to feed your pet is to give it specially balanced cat food. This may be canned, semi-moist or dry. The amount needed will vary with the weight of the cat and its way of life, but most packet or canned foods tell you the amount that you should offer.

◁ Cats usually choose to scratch trees or wooden posts. This helps to keep their claws short and warns other cats away by the marks that they make and the scent that they leave.

▽ You can provide your cat with an indoor scratching post made of a piece of wood. Tack an old piece of carpet around it to prevent the cat from damaging your furniture.

When you get your kitten, its mother should already have taught it how to use a litter box. If it does not know, put it in the box and, holding its front paws, make gentle digging movements with them.

Most kittens will understand, but if yours refuses, check that the box is clean and does not smell of another cat, as many cats will be put off by this. If it still refuses, swab any place that it uses with vinegar and put a clean box nearby.

Cats may mark the area that they think of as their own with urine and the smell from glands on their feet.

When a cat sharpens its claws on a piece of wood it is also spreading scent. Sometimes it will do this indoors, on a piece of furniture.

You can try to stop your cat from ruining your furniture by placing an indoor scratching post or plank close to the place that it has been using. You may have to spray the old "scratching" area with a new scent so that your cat won't keep using it any longer.

▽ You should stop your cat from getting on your bed or furniture. The best way to do this is to let it have a place that it knows is its own. If it has a cushion in a sunny corner it will usually be content to snooze there.

Cat hygiene

Most cats spend a good deal of time keeping themselves clean and tidy. They do this mostly by licking the coat so that their rough tongues pull out any loose hairs and remove any bits of dirt which may have caught in the fur.

Cats normally dislike being bathed, and although show cats are sometimes bathed it should not be necessary for your pet. You can help your cat to stay clean and healthy by inspecting its eyes, teeth and gums and grooming it regularly.

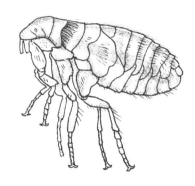

△ As you brush your cat look carefully at the skin to make sure that it has no parasites, such as fleas. This is particularly important after it has been in contact with other cats. Your vet will be able to tell you how to deal with these problems.

▷ Although kittens learn from their mothers how to groom themselves, you can help your pet with your grooming routine.

By regular brushing, you will prevent the cat from swallowing a lot of fur. This fur can cause fur balls to form in the animal's stomach if it is not removed.

You may also be able to prevent other health problems by noticing them at an early stage.

You should groom a short-haired cat by going over it from head to tail (not forgetting underneath the cat) with a stiff brush.

Long-haired cats must be groomed every day. You may find some tangles in their coats, which will need to be coaxed out gently with your fingers. Then use a wide-toothed metal comb and finally a brush, working against the direction of the fur, so that it stands out from the body.

▽ Your grooming kit should contain a variety of brushes and metal combs.

Playing with your cat

All kittens are playful and from the age of about three weeks begin to play with their mother and brothers and sisters. Their games are training for the life of a hunter – which is what all cats are at heart.

If you watch a kitten playing, you can see it practicing stalking and pouncing, which is the action it will

▽ Everyone in the family can enjoy watching and playing with a cat, although very young children can be rough and may get scratched. After playing, the cat will probably want to rest, perhaps by sitting on your lap and being stroked gently.

Many things can give your cat pleasure, but one of the best is to grow catnip – even a pot of it will do if you do not have a garden. Your cat will almost go into a trance, chewing and rolling in the plant. If you cannot grow catnip, you can buy toys already scented with catnip.

△ Cats enjoy exploring their territory and will often climb trees or on to roof tops. They have quick reflexes and are very agile.

use when it hunts a mouse. Or it may leap and swat something in the air, as if it were catching a bird, or it may scoop a ball or a feather from the ground as if it were flipping a fish from water.

As cats grow up they become less playful, although two or more cats will often play kittenish games. A cat does not need expensive toys. A cotton spool on elastic tied to a door handle will give it plenty of chance to play "bird swat." A piece of string and crumpled paper make a fine "mouse hunt" toy.

Some cats will retrieve balls – table tennis balls are probably the best. Watch your own cat and try to invent special games for it.

Cat health

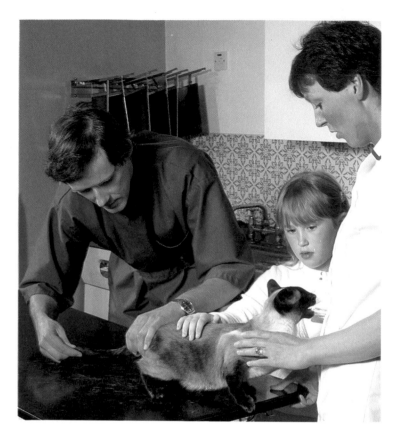

◁ A healthy cat looks glossy and contented. One reason that such an animal should visit the vet, other than for injection boosters, is that all cats, except those intended for breeding, should be neutered at about the age of five or six months.

If you keep your cat in clean conditions, feed it sensibly and groom it daily, it should remain healthy for most of its life. But cats may catch diseases. The worst are feline infectious enteritis and cat flu, both of which can be fatal. Mostly they may be prevented by vaccination. Your kitten should be taken to the vet for immunizing injections when it is about two months old.

Your cat will tell you itself if it is not feeling well, as it will become listless and unwilling to play. Its coat will look dull, its nose may run, its eyes may have an unfocused look and it will probably not want to eat.

If you notice any of these signs, take it to the vet, who should be able to deal with what is wrong before it becomes serious. Do not give your cat human medicine. Many things, such as aspirin, are dangerous for cats.

▽ When you groom your cat you should watch for skin conditions such as ringworm, parasites or damage caused by fighting. Road accidents are another reason for injuries. One way to try to prevent these is to keep your pet indoors at night.

Cats and kittens

Kittens are delightful animals, but many unwanted kittens are born and are destroyed or become strays. These animals are not cared for and can often pass on diseases to other cats that they meet.

△ You may have no idea that your cat is pregnant until she increases in size because of the babies growing inside her. Then she will probably have about two weeks to go before the birth.

Unless you have a pedigreed cat from which you wish to breed, the sensible thing is to have your cat neutered at the age of about five or six months.

It is not unkind to prevent a cat from having kittens – she keeps them for a very short time and does not remember them or miss them once they have gone.

A neutered tomcat is a far pleasanter pet, less smelly, less inclined to wander or to fight than one which is not neutered. If you have a female cat that has not been neutered be careful not to let her out when she is in heat, she is almost certain to mate with a roaming male.

▽ Cats normally give birth to their kittens with no trouble, but you must get the advice of a grownup and the help of a vet if your pet seems to be in distress. The babies are born blind and helpless, but their mother will care for them. Their eyes open by the time that they are ten days old. When they are four weeks old they are active kittens and you can start the process of weaning them (feeding more solid food in addition to their mother's milk). This should be complete by the time that they are eight to ten weeks old. Then you must find good homes for all of them.

Cats are creatures of habit and dislike having their routine broken. The best arrangement for your cat if you are away is to have a friend or neighbor looking after it in your house. If you cannot find somebody to do this, then you should take it to a local kennel.

If you are going away for a long time, and you are visiting a place where cats are welcome, you can consider taking your cat with you. Think very carefully before you do

△ A boarding kennel may ask to see your cat's vaccination certificates before they will accept it. Once there, your cat should be given a comfortable, warm sleeping place and exercise area. The people who are caring for it will need to know what its diet has been and the name of your vet. If they do not ask these questions, look for another place to leave your pet.

this. The journey will possibly be an ordeal for it and your pet might be better off in a good kennel. This can be quite expensive, so do get estimates before you make any final plans for your vacation.

Cats can often become unsettled after a move so, if you move to a new home you should shut your cat in a secure room when you arrive. Leave food, bed and a litter box with the cat, until all the removal's activity is over.

Don't let it out until you feel it's settled in the new house. When you first let it outside, go with it while it makes its first exploration.

△ If you take your cat with you on holiday, make sure that it does not stray away and become lost. Introduce it to the new area gradually and always stay close to your pet for the first few days.

Checklist

 Before you buy check:

1 That your family agrees.
2 That you have room to keep a cat.
3 That you can afford its food and vet's bills.
4 That you have time to look after it.
5 That you know a veterinarian.

 Remember daily:

1 To feed your cat each morning and evening.
2 To see that it always has fresh water to drink.
3 To wash its feeding and drinking dishes and any saucepans used to prepare its food.
4 To brush and comb it.
5 To clean its bedding.
6 To play with it.

 Remember weekly:

1 To check that you have enough food for the coming week.
2 To wash its bedding.
3 To check its gums, teeth and paws carefully to make sure that it is healthy.

 Remember yearly:

1 To have booster inoculations.
2 To take your cat to the veterinarian for its check-up.

Questions and answers

Q How long does a cat live?
A Many cats live for as long as 15 years. The oldest known cat survived for over 28 years.

Q Which cats make the best pets?
A The oriental short-haired, long-legged cats are often highly strung and so may be less suitable as family pets. European or American short-haired cats are easier to handle. Long-haired cats are often very placid, but they need a great deal of grooming.

Q Is it true that cats always fall on their feet?
A No. Although cats are very agile and can usually right themselves when they fall, they do not always do so and can hurt themselves.

Q Do all cats have fleas?
A No. But animals which are allowed to wander freely may catch fleas from other cats. You can get flea powders which will remove them from your cat's fur and by shaking and washing the cat's bedding frequently you can prevent fleas from becoming established in the house.

Q What is the cat's scientific name?
A *Felis domesticus.*

Index

PRINTED IN BELGIUM BY
proost
INTERNATIONAL BOOK PRODUCTION

636.8
POP
   Pope, Joyce
    Taking care of your
   cat

DATE DUE

	MAR 2 3 2012	
DEC 0 3 2012		
	AUG 0 9 2012	
	JAN 2 0 2012	

MAY 27 '99

27 2006

SEP 2 3 2011